The Taj Mahal

Other titles in this series

The Taj Mahal

GREAT STRUCTURES IN HISTORY

Rachel Lynette

KIDHAVEN PRESS

An imprint of Thomson Gale, a part of The Thomson Corporation

THOMSON
™
GALE

Detroit • New York • San Francisco • San Diego • New Haven, Conn.
Waterville, Maine • London • Munich

LIBRARY OF CONGRESS CATALOGING-IN-PUBLICATION DATA

Lynette, Rachel.
  The Taj Mahal / by Rachel Lynette.
    p. cm. — (Great structures in history)
  Includes bibliographical references and index.
  ISBN 0-7377-3154-0 (hard cover : alk. paper)
  1. Taj Mahal (Agra, India)—Juvenile literature. 2. Architecture, Islamic—India—Agra—Juvenile literature. 3. Agra (India)—Buildings, structures, etc.—Juvenile literature. I. Title. II. Series.
  NA6183.L95 2005
  726'.8'09542—dc22
                                        2004027927

CONTENTS

CHAPTER ONE

A Monument of Love

The Taj Mahal is one of the most beautiful structures in the world. Its massive onion-shaped dome and adjoining towers are covered by white marble. In bright sunlight the marble shines a gleaming white. At dawn and twilight it takes on softer, pink tones. The walls of the Taj Mahal are decorated with thousands of gems, elaborate carvings, and verses from the *Koran*. Beautiful gardens surround the building, which was built on the left bank of the Yamuna River near the city of Agra in northern India.

The Taj Mahal is the main part of a larger complex that includes other buildings, elaborate gardens, fountains, and reflecting pools. The complex covers forty-two acres. The entire complex is surrounded by a red sandstone wall.

When the Taj Mahal was built in the 1630s, this area was home to some of the richest people in India. Elaborate villas and palaces dotted the riverbanks along with beautiful gardens. In addition, the Red Fort is located within sight of the Taj Mahal. The Red Fort is a complex of palaces built in the mid 1500s. The builder of the Taj

Mahal, Shah Jahan, spent his childhood and later years in these palaces.

Shah Jahan was the fifth ruler of the Mogul Empire. The Moguls came from Central Asia. They conquered lands with their massive armies until they ruled the areas that are now Pakistan and Afghanistan and most of India. The Moguls ruled for more than 300 years, from 1526 to 1858. The Moguls were not kind to the common people. They treated them cruelly and taxed them heavily, keeping

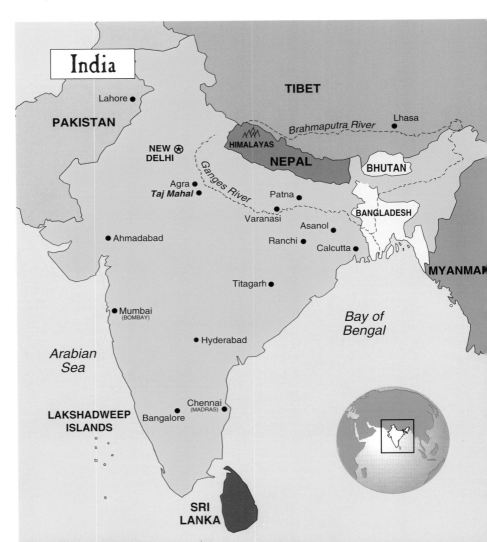

In this illustration, members of Shah Jahan's court pay a tribute of gold and silver equivalent to the Mogul ruler's weight.

them in poverty for generations. In contrast, the Moguls grew powerful and very wealthy.

Shah Jahan was one of the richest men in the world. He had many palaces spread across his land. It is said that he had hundreds of trunks full of precious gems, many tons of gold, and several gold thrones decorated with diamonds and emeralds. Historians describe him as a passionate, self-important man who had a keen interest in art and architecture. He was an excellent general and helped to increase the Moguls' lands and wealth in the many wars they fought. He was also devoted to his favorite wife, Mahal Mumtaz, for whom the Taj Mahal was built. Shah Jahan used his great wealth, power, and love of architecture to build his wife a magnificent tomb when she died nineteen years after they were married.

Jahan and Mumtaz

The story of why Shah Jahan built the Taj Mahal is one of love and sadness. It began in 1607 when Shah Jahan was only sixteen years old. He was not yet the emperor and was called Prince Khurram. The prince met a young girl named Arjumand Banu at the royal market. Arjumand was beautiful, kind, and well educated. She came from a wealthy family. Although they had spent only a few minutes together, the two fell in love that day.

The next day, Khurram asked his father, Emperor Jahangir, to allow him to marry the beautiful girl. His father agreed to arrange the marriage, but they had to wait five years to marry. They did not see or talk to each other during this time.

There were two reasons for this long engagement. Khurram's father wanted to use his son's marriage for his own political gain. Before Khurram married Arjumand, the prince was married to a princess from a royal Persian family. Muslim men were allowed four wives, so the marriage did not mean he could not wed Arjumand. The second reason they could not marry right away had to do with the stars.

In the Mogul Empire, the dates for royal weddings were set by astrologers. The astrologers looked to the positions of the stars and planets to determine the proper day for such important events. The astrologers did not deem the union between Khurram and Arjumand favorable until March 27, 1612.

On that day, a huge wedding procession wound its way from the Red Fort to Arjumand's home. There were elephants, musicians, dancers, and acrobats. The wedding ceremony took place at the bride's house, followed by a feast in honor of the newly married couple. On the wedding day, Emperor Jahangir gave his new daughter-in-law the name Mumtaz Mahal, which means "Chosen One of the Palace."

Although Khurram had other wives, Mumtaz Mahal remained his favorite as well as his constant companion. She traveled with him to military battles and advised him on important political matters. She was known for her compassionate nature and kindness to the poor. Over the nineteen years of their marriage, they had fourteen children. Seven of them lived beyond infancy.

Khurram was his father's favorite son and most important general. He won many battles that increased the Moguls' territory as well as their wealth. Toward the end of

Shah Jahan embraces his wife Mumtaz Mahal, as the two share a drink. Mumtaz Mahal was the shah's dearest companion.

his life, Jahangir gave his son the title Shah Jahan, which means "Ruler of the World." When the emperor died in 1627, Shah Jahan overcame the opposition of other family members to become the new emperor. He took the throne in February 1628.

Shah Jahan had been emperor for just three years when Mumtaz Mahal died giving birth to their fourteenth child.

In this painting, Shah Jahan holds his wife after she died giving birth to the couple's fourteenth child.

Shah Jahan had moved his court south to the town of Burhanpur for military purposes. After a day of directing troops, Jahan was called to Mumtaz Mahal's tent where she lay dying. No one knows exactly what Shah Jahan said to his wife in her last hour. According to legend, he promised to build her a magnificent tomb as a symbol of their love.

Mourning for Mumtaz Mahal

After Mumtaz Mahal's death, Shah Jahan was so overcome with grief that he did not come out of his rooms for seven days. He emerged looking weary and much older than his thirty-nine years. He lost his passion for battle and did not take pleasure in rich food, lavish clothes, music, or anything else that his great wealth could provide. Instead Shah Jahan turned his attention to building his wife's tomb in Agra.

Mumtaz Mahal's body was moved 435 miles (700km) from Burhanpur to Agra in a large funeral procession. Everyone in the procession wore white, which is the Muslim color of mourning. Thousands of soldiers accompanied the royal family on this journey. In Mumtaz Mahal's memory, huge amounts of food, silver, and gold were distributed to the poor along the way. The procession reached Agra in January 1632. Mumtaz Mahal's body was buried in a temporary grave near the site of what would one day be the Taj Mahal.

CHAPTER TWO

Building the Taj Mahal

Construction on the Taj Mahal began in 1632, a year after Mumtaz Mahal's death. Work continued for eleven years. Thousands of workers came from all over India as well as other parts of Asia and the Middle East to work on the emperor's tomb. Most were unskilled workers. However, there were also many gem cutters, goldsmiths, stone masons, **calligraphers**, and other artists. In all, more than twenty thousand people worked on the Taj Mahal.

The design of the grand tomb fell to a team of **architects**, engineers, and artists. These designers came from every corner of the empire. Each brought a unique style of architecture. Muslim, Hindu, and Persian styles of architecture all can be seen in the Taj Mahal, perfectly combined to form the beautiful tomb.

The outer design has many features commonly seen in Muslim style architecture. The Taj Mahal is **symmetrical**. This means that when viewed from the front, it looks the same on both sides. The central feature of the tomb is a large onion-shaped dome. It is surrounded by four smaller domes. The tomb sits on a large marble square called a **plinth**. At each corner of the plinth stands a tall, narrow tower called a **minaret**.

The inside of the Taj Mahal follows Persian styles of architecture. It is two stories high with a large octagon-shaped room in the center. This room contains the **cenotaphs**, or symbolic tombs, of Mumtaz Mahal and Shah Jahan. Their bodies are buried beneath this room. This central room is surrounded by sixteen rooms, eight on each floor.

The exterior of the Taj Mahal features elements common in Muslim architecture, including domes and minarets.

Transporting Materials

For the magnificent tomb, Shah Jahan ordered materials from all across the continent. The marble, as well as thousands of precious gems and other materials, were brought to Agra by a fleet of one thousand elephants. Hundreds of oxen, boats, and carts were also used. Bricks were made in thousands of kilns around Agra. Red sandstone was mined from local quarries. Great quantities of expensive blue-veined white marble were brought 200 miles (322km) from Makran. Beautiful shells and mother-of-

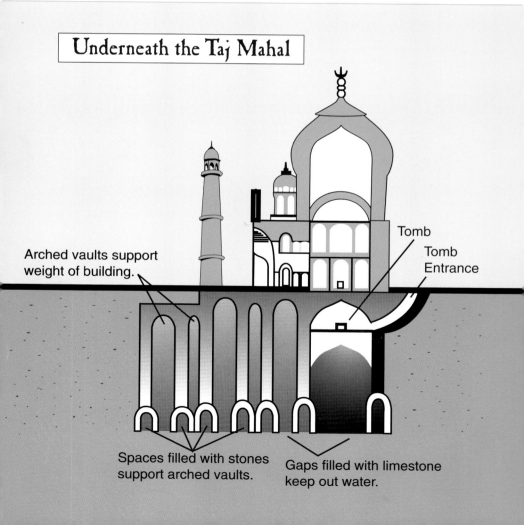

Underneath the Taj Mahal

Arched vaults support weight of building.

Tomb

Tomb Entrance

Spaces filled with stones support arched vaults.

Gaps filled with limestone keep out water.

pearl came from the Indian Ocean. Precious gems and gold came from all over the empire and from as far away as China.

A 10-mile (16-km) ramp made from dirt was built through Agra to transport the materials to the work site. The ramp sloped gradually so that even the heaviest loads of bricks or marble could be brought to the building site. From there, workers used a system of pulleys to lift the materials to where they were needed.

A Strong Foundation

While materials were being brought to the site, thousands of other workers were building the foundation of the tomb. The foundation of the Taj Mahal was very important. It would have to support a lot of weight. In addition, because it was built on the bank of a river, it had to be waterproof. The builders made sure that when the Yamuna River flooded in the **monsoon** season, the tomb would not be harmed.

The foundation covered an area as large as three football fields. Workers readied the site by digging several yards into the earth and then hauling all the dirt away. All this work had to be done by hand with simple tools.

The foundation had to keep the massive structure from sinking into the earth during the muddy monsoon season. This was done using an underground system of drainage pipes, wells, and arches. All of these helped keep water away from the structure and helped spread the building's great weight over a wide area.

The area beneath the foundation was then filled with stones and cemented together with mortar and covered with bricks. The bricks were painted with a special chemical to make them waterproof. It took three years to complete the foundation. However, the time and effort has proved well worth it. It is this ingenious foundation that has kept the Taj Mahal above ground for more than four hundred years.

The large platform, or plinth, that supports the Taj Mahal was built over the foundation. It is 208 yards (190m) long, 78 yards (71m) wide, and 9 yards (8m) high. It was made of stone and mortar and then covered with red sandstone. A smaller square plinth was constructed on top of the larger rectangular one. This smaller plinth was covered with white marble and built to support the main building.

Bricks and Marble

The Taj Mahal was first built from bricks and then covered with large slabs of perfectly cut and polished white marble. Unskilled workers made millions of bricks and brought them to the site in carts. Skilled bricklayers did the careful work of building the walls, one layer at a time. The bricks were treated with chemicals to make them strong and cemented together with strong mortar.

When a wall was complete, it was covered with white marble. Before the marble was even transported to the building site, it had to be cut into large, flat rectangles. This job was done by skilled masons using mallets and chisels. The marble was then polished smooth with sand. These giant slabs of perfectly polished marble were about 1.5 feet (46cm) thick and could weigh as much as 6 tons (5.4 metric tons). It took many workers and strong ropes

The walls of the Taj Mahal were first built of brick and then covered with slabs of perfectly cut and polished white marble.

Twelve thousand tons of marble slabs were used to build the Taj Mahal's enormous main dome, seen here behind one of the minarets.

and pulleys to position a slab of marble against the brick. Once it was in the correct position, it was held there with iron clamps until the mortar was dry.

The Dome

Once the walls were up, it was time for the biggest challenge of building the Taj Mahal: constructing the large double-shelled dome. The outer shell of the dome is 144 feet (44m) high, while the inner shell rises to only 81 feet (25m). The architects used this double-shell construction because they wanted the dome to look large and impressive on the outside. However, a dome that large would have overwhelmed the smaller rooms inside the tomb. That is why another, smaller dome was constructed under the first one.

It took 12,000 tons (10,886 metric tons) of marble slabs to build the dome. Each giant slab of marble had to be hoisted into exactly the right spot, as did all the mortar needed to cement it into place. Another, shorter ramp was built to transport the marble and other materials to the top of the dome. This ramp was 2 miles (3km) long. Once the materials were at dome level—about twenty-two stories by today's standards—they were lifted into place using ropes, pulleys, and crowbars.

After the large central dome was finished, the other four domes were constructed. The Taj Mahal was designed with many domes, half domes (or **iwans**), and arches. Aside from adding to the beauty of the structure, their rounded shape helped distribute the massive amount of weight of the building.

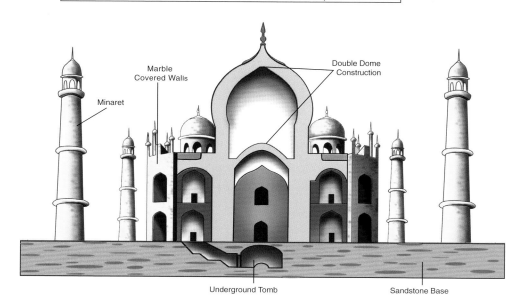

Structural Elements of the Taj Mahal

Marble Covered Walls

Double Dome Construction

Minaret

Underground Tomb

Sandstone Base

Minarets and Other Structures

After the main building was constructed, the four minarets were built. Each tower rises 138 feet (42m), making them just a little shorter than the central dome. The minarets are not perfectly straight. They were built angling slightly away from the tomb. That way if one of them were to fall over, it would fall away from the dome and not into it. Each minaret has two balconies. In the Muslim religion a minaret is used to call people to prayer. The Taj Mahal needed only one, but four were built to keep the building symmetrical.

Other, smaller buildings were constructed after the main structure was built. A **mosque** and the guesthouse were built to the sides of the tomb. These structures look identical from the outside, in keeping with the symmetry of the complex. A large main gate was built at the southern entrance to welcome visitors. The main gate was one of the last structures to be completed. However, the Taj Mahal complex was far from finished. The gardens, pools, and much of the decorations had yet to be completed.

CHAPTER THREE

Flowers, Fountains, and More

The Taj Mahal is beautiful from a distance. The graceful domes and symmetrical design make it look like a castle from a fairy tale. Visitors are often amazed by its architectural beauty. However, it is only when they come close to the monument that they can fully appreciate the massive work of art that is the Taj Mahal.

The Taj Mahal is decorated inside and out. Detailed carvings, jewels, paintings, and calligraphy can be found throughout the structure. Each decoration is a work of art by itself, but all together they make the Taj Mahal the biggest work of art in the world. Designed to enhance the tomb, the carvings and calligraphy adorn the walls, doorways, ceilings, and even the cenotaphs of the king and queen.

Carvings

The majority of the carvings in the Taj Mahal are of flowers. Delicate irises, tulips, daffodils, lilies, honeysuckles, and oleanders decorate many of the walls. In the Muslim religion, flowers are a symbol of paradise. There are thousands of flowers carved into the Taj Mahal because Shah Jahan wanted his wife's tomb to be a paradise on Earth.

The carvings were made using a method called **pietra dura**. The beautiful pietra dura carvings took a great deal of skill and time to create. First the design was drawn onto the marble with henna, a red-brown dye. Then expert carvers used different-sized chisels to carve out the design. It could take hours or even days to carve just a small section. Skilled gem cutters then carved precious and semiprecious stones to fit into the carvings. Turquoise, lapis, topaz, agate, jasper, amethyst, and jade were some of the

Intricate flower carvings like these make up much of the decoration on the Taj Mahal's interior and exterior walls.

more than forty varieties of stones used. The stones were carefully selected for their high quality and color. Once the stones were cut to the right shape, they were set into the marble carvings with putty and polished to a high shine. A single flower might contain as many as sixty different gems. The beautiful gems gave the carvings the appearance of real flowers.

Some of the most beautiful and detailed carvings are on the cenotaphs of the king and queen and on the octagon-shaped screen that surrounds them. The cenotaphs are made of pure white marble. The carvings on the two cenotaphs are similar to each other, although Shah Jahan's cenotaph was crafted many years after Mumtaz Mahal's. The 8-foot-tall (2.4m) lattice screen also made from white marble, filters the light to create a spiritual atmosphere and a misty appearance. It is decorated with elaborate pietra dura flowers, fruit, and vines. It took more than ten years to make this screen.

Calligraphy

A final and very important type of carving found on the Taj Mahal is calligraphy. Calligraphy is considered a high form of art in the Muslim religion. Twenty-two passages and fourteen entire chapters from the *Koran* are carved into the walls of the Taj Mahal.

The flowing Arabic letters that make up the calligraphy of the Taj Mahal were probably drawn by a man named Amanat Khan. He most likely supervised a team of stone carvers who helped complete the work. Khan must have been highly respected by Shah Jahan. He is the only artist

Black-marble calligraphy (inset) is beautifully carved into the walls of the Taj Mahal.

who worked on the Taj Mahal who was allowed to sign his work. Many historians believe he also selected the verses that appear on the walls from the *Koran*.

The calligraphy in and around the Taj Mahal is carved with black marble. The letters were first drawn onto the marble surface with henna. Then carvers chiseled out the graceful, overlapping letters. Stonecutters formed the same letters in black marble and set each piece into the white marble background. The result is a beautiful, flowing script.

Calligraphy can be found on the arched doorways and iwans of the Taj Mahal and in the guest house, mosque, and main gate. The letters were designed to look as if they are all the same size to someone standing on the ground. However, they actually are not the same size. Because things seen at a distance look smaller than things seen close up, Amanat Khan made the letters near the top of the arches bigger than those near the bottom. This makes them look as if they are all the same size.

Balance, proportion, and symmetry are all important themes in the Taj Mahal. All these ideas are carried into the design of the gardens, pools, and fountains that surround the structure.

Gardens and Plants

Similar to the Taj Mahal complex, the gardens that surround it were also designed to be symmetrical. They were divided into four identical square sections. Each garden was crossed by paths that divided them into four smaller quarters. Each of these quarters was further divided into sixteen flowerbeds. No one knows for sure what plants grew in these gardens during Shah Jahan's time. Reports from traveling Europeans suggest that the gardens were planted with many kinds of flowers including tulips, crocuses, and dahlias. There were also many fruit trees. Colorful, exotic birds were brought in to live in the trees. Shah Jahan wanted his wife's tomb to be a paradise on Earth. This was certainly reflected in the gardens.

Water was an important part of the Taj Mahal gardens. A great deal of water was needed to keep the gardens lush and green. Like every other part of the complex, the water features were designed not only to serve a purpose but also to enhance the overall beauty of the tomb. Two canals of water divide the gardens into four sections. They contain evenly spaced fountains. There is a square pool in the center where the two canals meet. The channel that runs from the tomb to the main gate perfectly reflects the Taj Mahal. The canals of water are thought to represent the *Koran*'s Four Rivers of Paradise.

The canals were supplied with water from the Yamuna River. Because the river was located below the Taj Mahal

Pools of water and flower gardens adorn the Taj Mahal complex. Water and flowers are symbols of paradise in Islam.

Taj Mahal Grounds

1) Main Gateway
2) Gardens
3) Taj Mahal
4) Mosque
5) Guest House

complex, the water had to be lifted. This was done with **purs**—buckets attached to ropes and pulled up and down by oxen. Using a series of purs, pipes, and storage tanks, large amounts of water from the river were brought to the gardens of the Taj Mahal. Once there, the water was transported through underground pipes to different places around the gardens. The water system is not only well designed but also well made. The main pipe for the system is buried 5 feet (1.5m) under a paved pathway and still works today.

The Taj Mahal Completed

Most historians think the Taj Mahal was completed in 1643, twelve years after Mumtaz Mahal died. Each year during construction, and for the rest of Shah Jahan's reign, lavish ceremonies, or urs, were held to mark the anniversary of Mumtaz Mahal's death. In the Muslim faith, a woman who dies in childbirth is thought of as a blessed martyr. The completed Taj Mahal complex became a place of pilgrimage for Muslims throughout the region, who came to be blessed by the dead queen. Even today the same prayers can be heard in the mosque as were heard hundreds of years ago when Shah Jahan wandered the gardens grieving for his beloved wife.

CHAPTER FOUR

Damage and Restoration

S hah Jahan was responsible for many beautiful works of architecture during his time as ruler of the Mogul Empire. None was as close to his heart as the Taj Mahal. After it was complete he kept it in excellent condition. Expensive Persian carpets and pillows were spread over the central chamber and changed several times a week. Incense burned constantly, and musicians played day and night. Two thousand soldiers stood guard around the complex. When repairs were needed, they were made immediately. All of this was paid for by Shah Jahan's subjects, who continued to live in poverty and many within sight of the magnificent tomb.

End of Shah Jahan's Rule

Shah Jahan's successor, his own son, did not share his father's affection for the Taj Mahal. Aurangzeb took over the Mogul Empire in 1658 by killing his three brothers who were rivals to the throne and imprisoning his father. Shah Jahan spent the last eight years of his life a prison-

Aurangzeb, Shah Jahan's son and successor, sits under a canopy surrounded by members of his court.

British officials meet with Indian rulers in this nineteenth-century illustration. Most Britons were not impressed with the Taj Mahal.

er in the Red Fort, where he could see the Taj Mahal from his window.

Shah Jahan died in 1666. Unlike his wife, he was not given a large funeral procession. Instead, Aurangzeb had the body quietly transported by boat to the Taj Mahal where it was entombed next to Mumtaz Mahal.

Aurangzeb was a bad ruler. His father had already done a lot of damage to the empire by taxing the people so much that they lived in poverty. He spent the money on expensive building projects and luxuries for the royal court. Aurangzeb made things worse by persecuting non-

Muslims and spending all the empire's money on wars that he could not win. By the end of his rule, the Moguls had no money and were hated by most of the people they ruled. In addition, Aurangzeb did not take care of the Taj Mahal. The beautiful tomb fell into disrepair. Thieves stole everything of value, and the gardens were overgrown with weeds.

The British

As the Moguls grew weaker, the British became stronger. They had been trading in India for many years. In 1858 the British took over the country and made it a British colony. The British expected the Indians to adopt British customs and ways of life. They scorned Indian art and architecture, including the Taj Mahal.

The British used the Taj Mahal for balls and parties. It became a favorite spot for picnics and for couples to meet. Often the British picnickers brought chisels to dig the precious gems out from the walls. Even the British governor-general of India saw possibilities for financial gain. He tore off a small section of marble and shipped it back to London to be sold at an auction. Fortunately no one wanted to buy the marble. If the marble had sold, he would have stripped the marble off the entire Taj Mahal.

Restoration of the Taj Mahal

Not all Britons showed such disrespect for Indian art and the Taj Mahal. Lord Curzon who governed the country in the early 1900s, loved Indian architecture and was especially

A workman climbs a bamboo ladder to reach a section of one of the Taj Mahal's walls in need of restoration.

enthralled with the Taj Mahal. He was appalled at how his countrymen had treated this magnificent building.

Curzon took on the large task of restoring the Taj Mahal. He employed native workers and had them trained to cut marble and repair the carvings and other artwork. Precious gems were replaced in the walls, cracks were repaired, and the marble was polished until it shone pure white once again. For the inside of the tomb, Curzon had a large brass lamp made in Egypt. He had the lamp hung in the center of the central dome, where it still hangs today.

Curzon also restored the gardens that surround the Taj Mahal. Trees and flowers were replanted. Walkways were cleared and repaved. Water channels were cleaned out, and the fountains were once again returned to working order. If Curzon had not taken on the job of restoring the Taj Mahal, tourists today might be visiting ruins rather than a beautiful symbol of love and Indian architecture.

Modern Challenges

India gained independence from Great Britain in 1947. In 1958 the Indian government created the Archaeological Survey of India. This organization was formed to oversee the Taj Mahal and other historic monuments in India. In 1983 the Taj Mahal became an official World Heritage Site. This means that like Stonehenge in England and the Great Wall in China, the Taj Mahal is considered one of the world's most important places. It also means that the Taj Mahal receives money from international sources to help keep it in good repair.

A section of marble from the Taj Mahal shows evidence of damage caused by pollution.

In 1998 several organizations began a three-year restoration project on the Taj Mahal. The project focused on the damage caused by water and pollution. It is very hot in Agra. The humidity levels are high, which means that there is a lot of moisture in the air. In addition, it rains almost constantly for three months every year. All this moisture has caused mold to grow, which can cause the marble to crack and wear away. The Taj Mahal also has problems with leaks. The domes have had leaks since they were first constructed. One of the most important parts of the restoration was applying waterproofing chemicals to stop the water damage.

Maintaining the Taj Mahal is not an easy job. Each year 2.5 million people come to see this magnificent monument, as many as 10,000 in a single day. The breath and sweat from all these people raise the humidity of the air inside the Taj Mahal. In addition, people often touch the walls, gems, and artwork, leaving the oil and dirt from their hands behind.

A construction worker restores a piece of stonework inside the Taj Mahal.

Indian tourists walk along the gardens of the Taj Mahal, one of the most-visited structures in the world.

Pollution has been another challenge, but the Indian government has done a lot to reduce this problem. Until recently there were many factories in the Agra area that burned coal. The soot from these factories was discoloring the marble of the Taj Mahal. Laws have been passed that ban this kind of pollution. Factories have either had to control their pollution output or shut down. Pollution from cars and trucks has also been reduced. Vehicles that use gasoline are no longer permitted within about 1,640 feet (500m) of the complex. Instead, people must use horses, camels, and battery-operated cars.

An Enduring Monument

The Taj Mahal is one of the most visited and well-known structures in the world. People take delight in the romantic story of its construction as well as its beauty and symmetry. Never has so grand a structure been built in honor of one woman.

It is a beautiful example of Mogul architecture and an important part of India's history. Now that steps are being taken to preserve and protect the monument people will be able to visit Mumtaz Mahal's tomb for generations to come.

Glossary

architect: People who design buildings or other large structures and advise in their construction.

calligraphers: Artists who produce beautiful handwriting.

cenotaphs: Tombs for people whose remains are buried somewhere else.

iwans: Vaulted halls open at one end.

Koran: The holy book of Islam.

minaret: The tower of a mosque used to call people to prayer.

monsoon: A period of heavy rainfall, especially in India.

mosque: A building in which Muslims worship.

pietra dura: A method of carving that involves setting carved pieces of precious gems into marble.

plinth: A low platform or base.

purs: A method of carrying water by using a bucket, rope, and oxen.

symmetrical: An object or design that is identical on both sides.

For Further Exploration

Books

Lesley A. DuTemple, *The Taj Mahal*. Minneapolis: Lerner, 2003. This book features interesting text and appealing pictures. Topics covered include the origins, construction, and gardens of the Taj Mahal and the fall of the Mogul Empire.

Joanne Mattern, *India*. Mankato, MN: Capstone, 2003. This informative book gives an overview of India including climate, wildlife, history, government, economy, and daily life. Each chapter begins with a Fast Facts section. Includes maps and a time line.

Patricia J. Murphy, *India*. Tarrytown, NY: Benchmark Books, 2003. This colorful book for younger readers provides interesting information about life in India. Includes fun activities, a glossary, and a section on how to count to ten in Hindi.

Christine Moorcroft, *The Taj Mahal: How and Why It Was Built*. Austin: Steck-Vaughn, 1998. This book gives basic information about the Taj Mahal and how it was built. It includes excellent color pictures, maps, a time line, and a glossary.

Web Sites

Agra (www.aviewoncities.com/agra.htm). This site (geared for travelers) features information about Agra, the Taj Mahal, and other interesting sites in the area. There are also many good pictures.

Taj Mahal—A Tribute to Beauty (www.angelfire.com/in/myindia/tajmahal.html). This site gives a brief history of the Taj Mahal and a link to dozens of excellent photographs.

A Tribute to Love: The Taj Mahal (http://library.thinkquest.org/J0112263/home.html?tqskip1=1). This ThinkQuest Web site was created by five fifth graders. The site includes a lot of interesting information about the Taj Mahal as well as an interactive quiz, glossary, and puzzles for printing.

Index

Picture Credits

About the Author

Rachel Lynette has written several other books for KidHaven Press, as well as dozens of articles on children and family life. She also teaches science to children of all ages. Rachel lives in the Seattle area in the Songaia Cohousing Community with her two children, David and Lucy; her dog, Jody; and two playful rats. When she is not teaching or writing she enjoys spending time with her family and friends, traveling, reading, drawing, rollerblading, and eating chocolate ice cream.